Every animal leaves traces of what it was;
only man leaves traces of what he created.

Jacob Bronowski

My Notes

This is my space to draw, paste, or write about the little things that say a lot about me.

It was really funny when:

_____

_____

_____

_____

_____

_____

_____

_____

_____

_____

_____

_____

_____

_____

A joke isn't a joke until someone laughs.

Michael Crawford

Notes on a fabulous new blog:

_____

_____

_____

_____

_____

_____

_____

_____

_____

_____

_____

_____

Drawing is still basically the same as it has been since prehistoric times. It brings together man and the world. It lives through magic.

Keith Haring

Use this space to bring out the creative genius in you.

PURE

My Thoughts

When I need inspiration, I think of:

_____

_____

_____

_____

_____

_____

_____

_____

_____

_____

_____

_____

_____

_____

_____

The most beautiful thing we can experience is the mysterious.
It is the source of all true art and science.

Albert Einstein

The most imaginative people are the most credulous, for to them everything is possible.

Alexander Chase

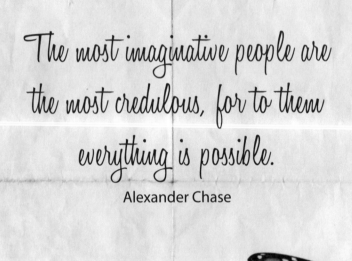

It took my breath away when I saw:

_____

_____

_____

_____

_____

_____

_____

_____

_____

_____

_____

_____

_____

_____

If I were a graffiti artist, I would put this all over walls:

Beauty is not caused. It is.

Emily Dickinson

Men live by forgetting—
women live on memories.

T. S. Eliot

This picture really warms my heart:

_____

_____

_____

_____

These songs are definitely on my playlist:

_____

_____

_____

_____

_____

_____

_____

_____

_____

_____

_____

_____

_____

_____

Happy times:

These things brought a smile to my face:

_____

_____

_____

_____

_____

_____

_____

_____

_____

_____

_____

_____

_____

_____

All I can say about life is,
Oh God, enjoy it!

Bob Newhart

It is important to express oneself... provided the feelings are real and are taken from your own experience.

Berthe Morisot

Design is a constant challenge to balance comfort with luxe, the practical with the desirable.

Donna Karan

Every now and then, I see a great design
that I want to tell my friends about:

_____

_____

_____

_____

_____

_____

_____

_____

_____

_____

_____

_____

_____

_____

BEAUTY

Painting is just another way of keeping a diary.

Pablo Picasso

When something catches my eye,
I should make a note of it:

_____

_____

_____

_____

_____

_____

_____

_____

_____

_____

_____

_____

_____

_____

_____

_____

My Ideas

Explore social networking and use this
space to write about new groups.

Use this space to note recent Twitter activity.

There is no must in art because art is free.

Wassily Kandinsky

I just had to say:
_____
_____
_____
_____
_____
_____
_____
_____
_____
_____
_____
_____
_____
_____
_____

A space to write:

_____

_____

_____

_____

_____

_____

_____

_____

_____

_____

_____

_____

_____

_____

_____

_____

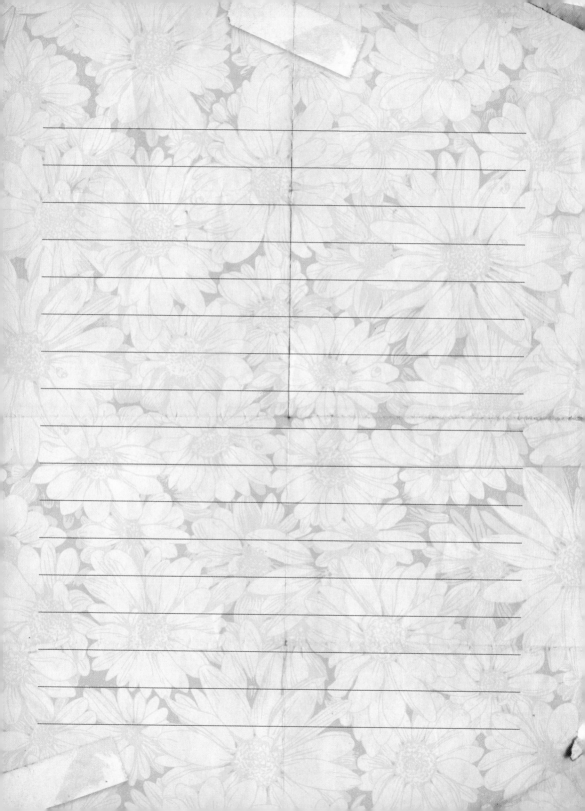

When I need inspiration, I think of:

_____

_____

_____

_____

_____

_____

_____

_____

_____

_____

_____

_____

_____

_____

Creativity takes courage.

Henri Matisse

When I hear these songs, I can't help singing along:

_____

_____

_____

_____

_____

_____

_____

_____

_____

_____

_____

_____

_____

_____

_____

*Music is meaningless noise unless
it touches a receiving mind.*

Paul Hindemith

A blank wall needs some graffiti!

I'm hoping these wishes come true:

_____

_____

_____

_____

_____

_____

_____

_____

_____

_____

_____

_____

If I could say it in words, there would be no reason to paint.

Edward Hopper

Tell your followers on Twitter:

_____

_____

_____

_____

_____

_____

_____

_____

_____

_____

_____

_____

_____

_____

A photo opportunity presented itself!

You can do anything in this world
if you are prepared to take the consequences.

W. Somerset Maugham

Sketch or doodle—the choice is yours!

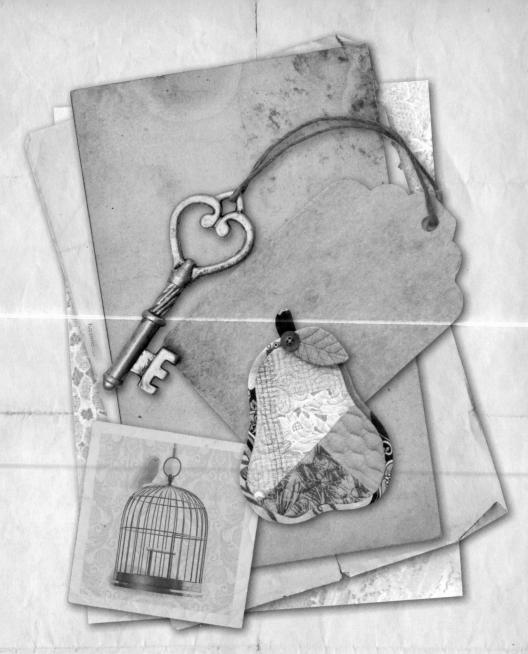

A thing of beauty is a joy forever: its loveliness increases; it will never pass into nothingness.

John Keats

Some things are too beautiful not to share.

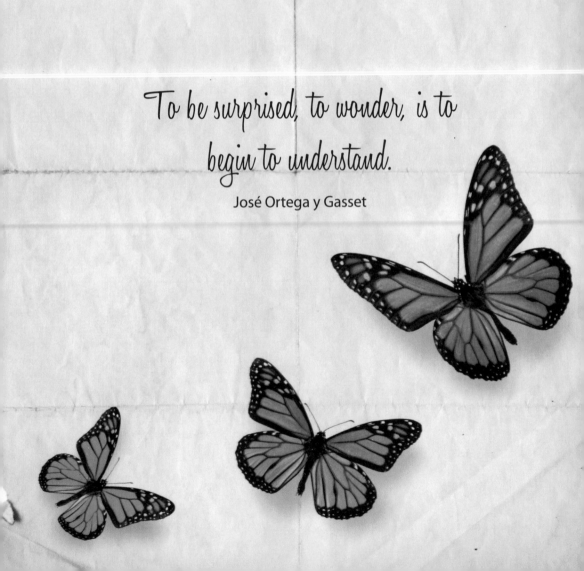

To be surprised, to wonder, is to begin to understand.

José Ortega y Gasset

This really inspired me:

The proper study of mankind is books.

Aldous Huxley

Before the year is over, I must read these books:

_____

_____

_____

_____

_____

_____

_____

_____

_____

_____

_____

_____

_____

_____

My Doodle Wall

ENJOY

I could watch these movies over and over again:

_____

_____

_____

_____

_____

_____

_____

_____

_____

_____

_____

_____

_____

_____

When I see this photograph, I smile.

We all have our time machines.
Some take us back, they're called memories.
Some take us forward, they're called dreams.

Jeremy Irons

These Tweets really made my day:

_____

_____

_____

_____

_____

_____

_____

_____

_____

_____

_____

_____

_____

Use this space to feel inspired.

I begin with an idea and then it becomes something else.

Pablo Picasso

The most gifted members of the
human species are at their creative
best when they cannot have their own way.

Eric Hoffer

An exciting new blog!

This caught my eye:

LIFE

I found a long-lost friend on Facebook:

If I were an artist, I would paint:

_____

_____

_____

_____

_____

_____

_____

_____

_____

_____

_____

_____

A work of art which did not begin
in emotion is not art.

Paul Cézanne

*There are flowers everywhere for those
who bother to look.*

Henri Matisse

This is your sketchpad.

I'm inspired by:

_____

_____

_____

_____

_____

_____

_____

_____

_____

_____

_____

_____

_____

_____

_____

_____

I couldn't stop smiling when:

_____

_____

_____

_____

_____

_____

_____

_____

_____

_____

_____

_____

_____

_____

_____

When people are smiling, they are most receptive to almost anything you want to teach them.

Allen Funt

I really should:

I can't stop singing this song!

_____

_____

_____

_____

_____

_____

_____

_____

_____

_____

_____

_____

*The heart of the melody can never
be put down on paper.*

Pablo Casals

Use this space to draw, paste, or paint the things that excite you.

I laughed so much when:

_____

_____

_____

_____

_____

_____

_____

_____

_____

_____

_____

_____

_____

_____

Don't be an art critic, but paint,
there lies salvation.

Paul Cézanne

A dream you dream alone is only a dream.
A dream you dream together is reality.

John Lennon

Paint or sketch, you decide.

This grabbed my attention:

_____

_____

_____

_____

_____

_____

_____

_____

_____

_____

_____

_____

_____

_____

The awareness of our own
strength makes us modest.

Paul Cézanne

Must-see movies:

This is a great design:

I travel a lot;
I hate having my life disrupted by routine.
Caskie Stinnett

If I had an around-the-world ticket, I'd go to:

_____

_____

_____

_____

_____

_____

_____

_____

_____

_____

_____

_____

_____

_____

_____

Something to try:

In order to succeed, your desire for
success should be greater than
your fear of failure.

Bill Cosby

I'd like to sketch:

_____

_____

_____

_____

_____

_____

_____

_____

_____

_____

_____

_____

_____

_____

_____

I'm reminded of a song:

Everyone thinks of changing the world,
but no one thinks of changing himself.

Leo Tolstoy

It's new, it's exciting!

I will always remember this:

_____

_____

_____

_____

_____

_____

_____

_____

_____

_____

No man and no force can abolish memory.

Franklin D. Roosevelt

MEMORY

Paint or sketch something you love.

A few things to wish for:

_____

_____

_____

_____

_____

_____

_____

_____

_____

_____

_____

_____

_____

_____

I am inspired by:

_____

_____

_____

_____

_____

_____

_____

_____

_____

_____

_____

_____

_____

_____

_____

_____

I don't really care who gets their inspiration from where, it's the end results that count.

Robert Lloyd

Make a note of it.

_____

_____

_____

_____

_____

_____

_____

_____

_____

_____

_____

_____

_____

_____

Sadness is almost never anything but a form of fatigue.

André Gide

There was never a night or a problem that could defeat sunrise or hope.

Bern Williams

Things to hope for:

_____

_____

_____

_____

_____

_____

_____

_____

_____

_____

_____

_____

_____

_____

I must be strong.

BRAVE

I'm remembering these lyrics:

_____

_____

_____

_____

_____

_____

_____

_____

_____

_____

_____

_____

_____

_____

_____

_____

I stopped in my tracks when I saw:

Repetition does not transform a lie into a truth.

Franklin D. Roosevelt

A new blog to enjoy:

This amazing design caught my eye:

_____

_____

_____

_____

_____

_____

_____

_____

_____

_____

_____

_____

Design is a funny word.
Some people think design means how it looks.
But of course, if you dig deeper,
it's really how it works.

Steve Jobs

A Blank Canvas

Hopes and Dreams

Beauty awakens the soul to act.

Dante Alighieri

A space to note the things that inspire me:

_____

_____

_____

_____

_____

_____

_____

_____

_____

_____

_____

_____

_____

_____

Use this space to note your first glimpse of something special:

_____

_____

_____

_____

_____

_____

_____

_____

_____

_____

_____

_____

_____

_____

_____

This Facebook wall is like no other:

_____

_____

_____

_____

_____

_____

_____

_____

_____

_____

_____

_____

_____

One day, I'll:

*My mother taught me about the power
of inspiration and courage, and she did it
with a strength and a passion that
I wish could be bottled.*

Carly Fiorina

Everyone has a muse:

These are a few of my favorite things:

_____
_____
_____
_____
_____
_____
_____
_____
_____
_____
_____
_____
_____
_____
_____
_____
_____
_____

This is my space.

All men are creative but few are artists.

Paul Goodman

*The pleasure of all reading is
doubled when one lives with another
who shares the same books.*

Katherine Mansfield

A book to recommend:

_____

_____

_____

_____

_____

_____

_____

_____

_____

_____

_____

_____

_____

A space to think:

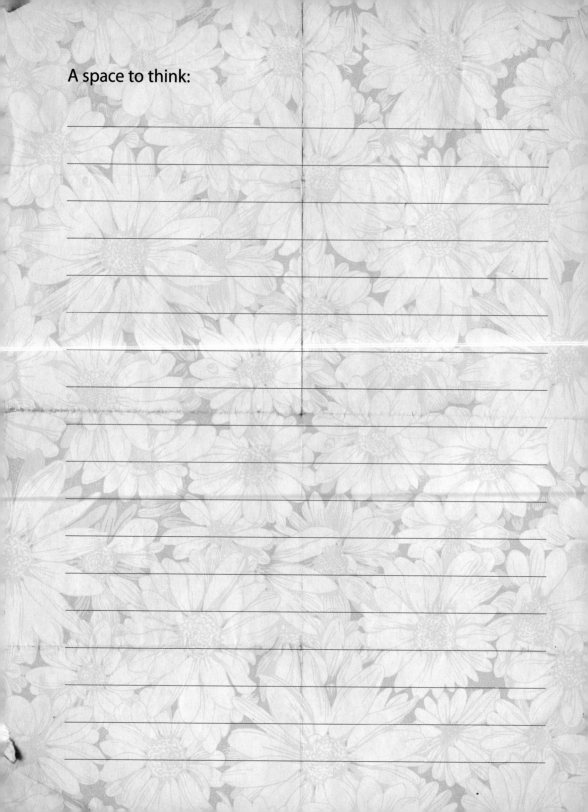

A song that makes me dance: